MW00452558

JOURNAL

PETER PAUPER PRESS, INC.
WHITE PLAINS, NEW YORK

PETER PAUPER PRESS
Fine Books and Gifts Since 1928

OUR COMPANY

In 1928, at the age of twenty-two, Peter Beilenson began printing books on a small press in the basement of his parents' home in Larchmont, New York. Peter—and later, his wife, Edna—sought to create fine books that sold at "prices even a pauper could afford."

Today, still family owned and operated, Peter Pauper Press continues to honor our founders' legacy—and our customers' expectations—of beauty, quality, and value.

Designed by Louis Comfort Tiffany, the leaded-glass window
Magnolias and Irises (ca. 1908) was created for the Frank family of New York City.

Anonymous Gift, in memory of Mr. and Mrs. A. B. Frank, 1981,
the Metropolitan Museum of Art, New York, NY.
This image is used courtesy of the museum (accession no. 1981.159).

Copyright © 2018
Peter Pauper Press, Inc.
202 Mamaroneck Avenue
White Plains, NY 10601 USA
All rights reserved
ISBN 978-1-4413-2883-0
Printed in China
14 13 12 11 10 9 8 7

Visit us at www.peterpauper.com